THE
POWER
OF
PRAISE

30 Days of Transformative Praise That Last a Lifetime

DR. MAKISHA DAVIS

Printed in the United States of America
ISBN: 978-1-965441-04-6

CONTENTS

ACKNOWLEDGEMENT

I would like to first thank God for walking with me and giving me the insight through the Holy Spirit to motivate and encourage others to ignite their praise to Him. I want to thank my husband, Kendall Davis, who has inspired me to move forward in the calling of God. I will always cherish these words in my heart "You are the most victorious woman I know". I want to dedicate this book to those who have encountered life disparities that have caused you to diminish your praise to God. He truly loves you and is with you as you travel through life.

PREFACE

This book aims to motivate believers to restore their praise to God in all areas of their Christian journey, particularly during times of crisis. In these challenging moments, it becomes crucial to remember the power of worship and gratitude, which can uplift the spirit and provide strength. It's important to understand that by praising God, we can triumph in our struggles and become victorious through Christ Jesus. The journey of faith requires us to acknowledge God through our praise. This allows us to welcome Him into our lives and be led by His calm as we journey. *For an enjoyable experience while reading this book, after you have engaged with the daily content, take a moment to read the chapter of the daily scripture in the Bible. Use the praise reflection to note any additional praises that resonate with you from the chapter. Spend a few moments reflecting on your reading, then transition to the glory moment setting to capture what flows from your heart. Finally, wrap up your day's experience by scanning the QR code that will guide you into a moment of praise.* It is my hope that you meet God in new ways through this 30-day interaction. Let the Holy Spirit lead you as you embark upon this excursion. May God bless you richly.

Day 1

EVERY PRAISE

Let everything that has breath praise the Lord.
Praise the Lord!

L et everything that has breath praise the Lord. In this scripture
from the Bible, the term "breath" translates to "Neshamah" in
Hebrew. This word primarily refers to the breath of life—the
vital force that animates living beings, as referenced in Genesis 2:7.
It is often associated with the divine breath that God imparts to hu-
mans. The Bible presents this scripture not as a mere suggestion but
as a command to humanity. Praise, described as "Halal" in Psalm
150:6, means to boast to God through singing. We see this theme
of praise throughout the book of Psalms. This act of praising is particularly significant for believers, especially when facing the diverse
challenges of life. Through praise, individuals can find strength and
solace, transforming their struggles into opportunities for spiritual

THE POWER OF PRAISE | 1

growth. Ultimately, the act of glorifying God serves as a reminder of His presence and love, encouraging believers to remain steadfast in their faith.

Praising God in adversity invites His presence and establishes a kingdom focus in various situations. Praise fosters hope that relies on faith in the Spirit, helping to cultivate a victorious mindset despite natural circumstances. Such praises enable believers to become overcomers through Jesus Christ. Additionally, praise assists us in forming spiritual patterns that allow for consistent communion with God. We offer Him praise during both the highs and lows of our lives, regardless of our feelings. God created us to praise Him. In doing so, we not only acknowledge His sovereignty but also align our hearts with His purpose. This continual act of worship transforms our perspective and empowers us to navigate life's challenges with grace and resilience. Let's take a moment today to use our divine breath to offer Him praise. (HALLELUJAH) **Let us praise God!**

Every Praise !

PRAISE REFLECTION

_____

_____

_____

_____

_____

_____

_____

_____

_____

GLORY MOMENTS

_____

_____

_____

_____

_____

_____

_____

_____

_____

_____

Day 2

PSALM 23

P S A L M   2 3 : 1 - 6

The LORD is my shepherd...

L ife takes us on a journey filled with various pathways. We make numerous choices, yet I have discovered that God is always present. Psalm 23 illustrates the guiding hand of God in the life of someone willing to follow Him. The first decision highlighted is the acknowledgment of God's role in the lives of believers. The Psalmist begins with the declaration, "The Lord is my Shepherd." The term "shepherd" is translated from the Hebrew word "RA'AH," which means one who feeds, tends, and protects the flock. This imagery emphasizes the deep relationship between God and His children, displaying His commitment to their well-being. By recognizing Him as our shepherd, we invite His guidance and care into every aspect of our lives, fostering a sense of security and purpose.

The Lord gives us everything we need. His protection keeps us safe and gives us the confidence that we don't have to be afraid of difficult times. In moments of uncertainty, we can lean on our faith, knowing that we are never truly alone. This assurance empowers us to face challenges with courage and resilience. His supply ensures our sustenance, and it is our responsibility to consume what He provides. By embracing His provision, we can cultivate gratitude, recognizing that each blessing strengthens our spirit. As we share these gifts with others, we create a ripple effect of hope and support in our communities. We feel fulfilled when we do what God created us to do. God gets the glory from our lives because of these things that happen. Therefore, we thank Him for being a good shepherd. We recognize that in every challenge, there is an opportunity for growth and deeper faith. Trusting in His guidance allows us to navigate life's uncertainties with grace and assurance. **Let us praise God!**

Psalm 23

PRAISE REFLECTION

_____
_____
_____
_____
_____
_____
_____
_____
_____

GLORY MOMENTS

_____
_____
_____
_____
_____
_____
_____
_____
_____
_____

Day 3

MAGNIFIED PRAISE

PSALM 69:30

I will praise the name of God with a song;
I will magnify him with thanksgiving.

L ife presents us with challenges and obstacles that we must overcome to fulfill our purpose, and God is not surprised by this. He has empowered us to praise Him even amidst our difficult circumstances. In these times, our praise should be magnified above our situations. When we do this, it increases our faith and encourages us to reflect on God's Word and His goodness. This reflection leads us to songs of thanksgiving and spiritual declarations. When we sing with the Word of God combined with faith, it creates a spiritual weapon that calls for God's assistance and brings about victory. We must understand that our praise is our weapon, and it fights for us.

The Bible provides an account in 2 Chronicles 20:20-23, where the Ammonites approached King Jehoshaphat to declare war. In response, he encouraged the people to have faith and praised God. King Jehoshaphat appointed several men to sing to God, and they sang, "Give thanks to the Lord; His love endures forever." God acted on their behalf, granting King Jehoshaphat victory over the Ammonites. Psalm 22:3 tells us that God dwells in the praises of His people. It is through our praises, combined with faith in God, that we enhance our ability to endure various challenges and achieve victory. **Let us lift our praises to God today!**

Magnify The Lord

PRAISE REFLECTION

_____

_____

_____

_____

_____

_____

_____

_____

_____

_____

GLORY MOMENTS

_____

_____

_____

_____

_____

_____

_____

_____

_____

_____

Day 4

MY HALLELUJAH

Revelation 19:1

*After this I heard what sounded like the roar of a great
multitude in heaven shouting: "Hallelujah! Salvation
and glory and power belong to our God.*

Hallelujah is known as the highest praise, as it is directed to God for His wondrous presence and works here on earth and in the heavens. The word "Hallelujah" carries the same meaning throughout the Bible, which means "Praise ye the Lord." This declaration cements the deep reverence and gratitude that we as believers express in praise. It serves as a reminder of the divine connection between God and humanity, and it brings joy and hope in the hearts of those who utter it. This powerful expression transcends language and culture, uniting people in faith and devotion to God. Whether sung in a congregation or whispered in solitude,

"Hallelujah" embodies the essence of praise, fostering a spirit of unity and shared purpose as a body of one.

The proclamation of Hallelujah also assists us in realigning our focus on God as we endure hardships, provoking spiritual growth as we draw closer to Him and He draws closer to us. Our relationship with God empowers us to face challenges with renewed strength and resilience. As we embrace our faith in God, we find comfort in the knowledge that we are never alone in our struggles. The word of God encourages us to rely on His strength and wisdom as He guides us through life's challenges. When we surrender our struggles to Him, we find peace and renewed purpose in our journey. This newfound clarity allows us to approach each day with hope and determination. Trusting in His plan, we can navigate uncertainties with confidence, knowing that every trial is an opportunity for growth. Revelation 19:1 shows us that God brings victory while also judging those who go against His will. We can shout Hallelujah for our victories because, as children of the Most High God, we know that His love and guidance are always with us. **Let us praise God!**

You Deserve It

PRAISE REFLECTION

_____

_____

_____

_____

_____

_____

_____

_____

_____

_____

GLORY MOMENTS

_____

_____

_____

_____

_____

_____

_____

_____

_____

_____

Day 5

VICTORIOUS PRAISE

1 CORINTHIANS 15:57

*But thanks be to God! He gives us the victory
through our Lord Jesus Christ.*

Thanksgiving God is embedded in our praise and leads us into victories that bring God glory. These victories remind us of the blessings we often take for granted and encourage us to share our gratitude with others. In doing so, we strengthen our faith and inspire those around us to recognize the goodness of God in their lives. This gratitude brings about a hope that causes us to praise God despite difficult situations. This hope gives us strength, allowing us to face challenges with a spirit of thanksgiving. As we cultivate this attitude, we become beacons of light for others, demonstrating that even in adversity, there is always a reason to celebrate and give God thanks. By sharing our experiences and the blessings we encounter, we encourage others to seek the positive aspects in their lives. Having a heart of thanksgiving toward God fosters unity among believers, where faith flourishes and love prevails even in the darkest times.

Paul reminds us that gratitude is essential to the victories won on our behalf through our Lord Christ Jesus. This attitude of thankfulness enriches our spiritual journey and strengthens our relationship with God. By recognizing the victorious blessings in our lives, we cultivate a deeper sense of joy. This joy not only uplifts our spirits but also inspires those around us to acknowledge the victories of God in their lives. In sharing our gratitude to God and before others, we create a ripple effect that is grounded in faith and appreciation. It is vital to return a praise of thanksgiving to the Lord for giving us wisdom and insight in the midst of battle. As well as standing with us during our trials, He equips us with the strength to persevere. This unwavering support encourages us to trust in His plan, which often unfolds in ways we may not immediately understand. Through faith in God, we find the courage to face the unknown, allowing us to grow and learn from each encounter. Therefore, we praise and give thanks to God in all things. **Let us praise God!**

We are Victorious

PRAISE REFLECTION

_____

_____

_____

_____

_____

_____

_____

_____

_____

_____

GLORY MOMENTS

_____

_____

_____

_____

_____

_____

_____

_____

_____

_____

Day 6

BRINGING FORTH GLORY

PSALM 72:19

Blessed be His glorious name forever!
Let the whole earth be filled with His glory!
Amen and amen.

We were created to bring God glory; this means that there is a reflector in us that shines God's glory back to Himself. This reflection enhances our relationship with Him and serves as a testament to His greatness in the world around us. As we embrace our purpose, we become vessels of His love and light, inspiring others to seek His presence. Our lifestyle reflects His holiness, displaying His glory and inspiring praise from the deepest depths of our spirit. This allows us to become intimate with God as His dear children. Through this intimacy, we learn to trust Him more fully and align our desires with His will. Each moment spent in His presence transforms us, enabling us to live out our faith authentically and share His message of hope with others.

King Solomon encourages us to bless His glorious name forever and let the whole earth be filled with His glory! In doing so, we participate in a timeless celebration of His majesty and grace. May our hearts resonate with praise, echoing the beauty of His creation throughout all generations. As we lift our voices in unison, let us inspire others to join in this divine chorus, recognizing God's splendor that surrounds us. Together, we can create a harmonious symphony of praise that transcends our differences and unites us in faith. Each note of gratitude adds to the richness of this eternal song. **Let us praise God!**

Glorious

PRAISE REFLECTION

_____
_____
_____
_____
_____
_____
_____
_____
_____
_____

GLORY MOMENTS

_____
_____
_____
_____
_____
_____
_____
_____
_____
_____

Day 7

BLESSED THE LORD

PSALM 34:1

I will bless the Lord at all times;
His praise shall continually be in my mouth.

The Psalmist David was regarded as a man after God's heart. His writings in the book of Psalms demonstrates his reputation as a praiser. King David knew how to approach the King of Glory. His method of approaching God through praise helped him overcome many difficult situations. We can draw inspiration from Psalm 34:1, where David begins this chapter with praise, despite his unique circumstances. This Psalm opens with "I will bless the Lord at all times." The word "bless" is "Barak" in Hebrew, which means to "adore on bending knees." Adopting this posture signifies a position of surrender, where one pays homage to the one that rules, and they serve. David further declares that he will remain in his current position as he praises God.

Praising God while maintaining a surrendered position allows us to remain steadfast until He shows up for us. In this state of surrender, we cultivate patience and trust, understanding that His timing is perfect. This attitude deepens our faith and encourages us to find joy in the journey, even when answers seem distant. While we wait, we can find strength in our relationship with God, understanding that He is consistently working in the background for our benefit. Taking this posture of praise allows us to assume the right position of respect for God, whom we serve. It reminds us that every moment of waiting is an opportunity for growth and reflection. Embracing this mindset not only fortifies our resolve but also helps us to appreciate the blessings that unfold along the way. Such praise allows the King of Glory, who is the King of Glory, the Lord strong and mighty, and the Lord mighty in battle (Ps. 24:1) to enter our hearts. As we cultivate this attitude of gratitude, we become more attuned to His divine presence in our lives. **Let us praise God!**

Bless the Lord

PRAISE REFLECTION

_____

_____

_____

_____

_____

_____

_____

_____

_____

_____

GLORY MOMENTS

_____

_____

_____

_____

_____

_____

_____

_____

_____

_____

Day 8

NEW SEASON

PSALM 144:9

I will sing a new song;
On ten string lyre I will make music for you.

The phrase "I will sing to You a new song" refers to a new way of praising God. A "new song" frequently signifies a new act of God's deliverance or a new revelation of Him in a biblical context. These expressions can manifest in various ways, ranging from sincere petitions to artistic creations, each of which serves as confirmation of the ongoing relationship between us and God. Embracing this concept strengthens one's faith and motivates others to investigate their own distinctive devotional practices. A lyre, another term for "harp of ten strings," refers to a specific musical instrument employed in ancient Israelite prayer. The ten-stringed harp offers a complete and harmonious sound, representing the totality of praise presented to God. This instrument served as a tool for worship and symbolized the depth of human expression through music. Its melodies were believed to elevate the spirit and connect the faithful to God.

During a new season, we have opportunities to elevate our praise to God on a deeper level, especially since He has brought us through the previous season. This fresh beginning invites us to reflect on our journey and express gratitude for the lessons learned. As we engage in praise, we can embrace the anticipation of growth and transformation that lies ahead. Our hearts can be filled with hope as we look forward to the new experiences and challenges that will shape us. By remaining open to His guidance, we can foster a spirit of joy and strength, ready to embrace all that this season has to offer. Let us express a new form of praise today for this new season in our lives. **Let us praise God!**

New Season

PRAISE REFLECTION

_____
_____
_____
_____
_____
_____
_____
_____
_____

GLORY MOMENTS

_____
_____
_____
_____
_____
_____
_____
_____
_____
_____

Day 9

GOD'S PRESENCE

PSALM 16:11

*You make known to me the path of life; you will fill me with joy
in your presence, with eternal pleasures at your right hand.*

Have you ever found yourself in a profound moment of distress, experiencing tremendous struggle and longing for the presence of God after countless questions through prayer? In these moments, when we feel the presence of God, our hearts transition from despair to joy. This change may be a strong reminder of how praise can help us overcome our doubts and fears. When we accept that spiritual connection, we frequently develop a new feeling of purpose and optimism that helps us confront our problems with strength. The presence of God brings a freedom that breaks the chains of adversity in our lives. This profound liberation enables us to reflect on God's goodness while offering Him our highest praise. This praise stems not from what we see in our current condition but from our understanding that the God we serve will always be with us and will never abandon us. Reflecting on this concept encourages us to examine our lives and recognize how God has consistently been present.

The psalmist highlighted that God is aware of our life journey, and we must keep in mind that our praise reflects His glory. The Bibles indicate that the joy of the Lord is our strength. (Nehemiah 8:10) As He receives glory from our praise, we gain strength. This act of praise not only fortifies personal convictions but also becomes a powerful testimony to God's unwavering faithfulness. His unfailing faithfulness serves as an anchor of praise, drawing others into His presence to experience His love and grace. **Let us praise God!**

Presence of the Lord!

PRAISE REFLECTION

_____

_____

_____

_____

_____

_____

_____

_____

_____

_____

GLORY MOMENTS

_____

_____

_____

_____

_____

_____

_____

_____

_____

_____

Day 10

UPLIFTED HAND

PSALM 63:4

I will praise you as long as I live;
and in your name I will lift up my hands.

We see here in Psalm 63:4 King David makes a declaration to God regarding his continual praise in acknowledgement of His great name. This commitment reflects David's deep understanding of the importance of praise and thanksgiving in his relationship with the Lord. His example encourages us to cultivate a similar attitude of reverence and appreciation in our lives. David does this through his symbolic praise of "Yadah", which means to lift your hands to God with gratitude in Hebrew. By expressing his devotion in such a tangible way, David demonstrates how physical acts of praise can enhance our spiritual connection. This call to action invites us to engage wholeheartedly in our own expressions of faith, reminding us that our gestures can reflect the depth of our love and commitment to God.

In our lives, there are times when circumstances cause us to use body gestures that God interprets. These gestures serve as powerful symbols of our inner feelings, transcending words and conveying our true intentions. Whether it's a moment of surrender, gratitude, or worship, our physical expressions can deepen our relationship with God. These moments invite us to be more attuned to our spiritual journey, encouraging us to embrace authenticity in our praise to God. By recognizing the significance of our actions, we can foster a more profound connection that resonates within our hearts and inspire those around us to do the same. **Let us praise God!**

We Lift Our Hands

PRAISE REFLECTION

_____

_____

_____

_____

_____

_____

_____

_____

_____

_____

GLORY MOMENTS

_____

_____

_____

_____

_____

_____

_____

_____

_____

_____

Day 11

PRAISES TO GOD

HEBREWS 13:15

*Through Jesus, therefore, let us continually
offer to God a sacrifice of praise,
the fruit of lips that confess His name.*

Have you ever wanted to praise God but found it challenging? In these times, we must turn to Jesus, who has perfected praise. Through Him, we can express our gratitude, worship, and love, even when our hearts feel heavy. Embracing His presence allows us to find the strength to lift our voices and celebrate His goodness. In moments of struggle, we can remember that our faith is a source of comfort and hope. Hope serves as a constant reminder that we are never alone. By placing our trust in God through faith, we allow Him to turn our trials into testaments of His grace and mercy. In keeping our focus on His unwavering love, we can overcome our doubts and distractions and fully engage in heartfelt praise.

In Old Testament Jewish culture, sacrifices were essential and a form of worship; however, praise is characterized in this verse as a sacrifice. This suggests that praise is a precious sacrifice to God, requiring intentionality and sometimes a personal price, particularly in difficult circumstances. This understanding encourages us to approach our worship with sincerity and dedication, recognizing that even in our trials, our praise can be a powerful testament to our faith. When we praise God in difficult times, we honor Him and improve our own spiritual endurance. This act of worship can transform our perspective of our current situation, reminding us of His faithfulness and the hope that lies beyond our current struggles. **Let us praise God!**

To Our God

PRAISE REFLECTION

_____
_____
_____
_____
_____
_____
_____
_____
_____
_____

GLORY MOMENTS

_____
_____
_____
_____
_____
_____
_____
_____
_____
_____

Day 12

HOSANNA

MARK 11:10

*Blessed is the kingdom of our father David that is coming
in the name of the Lord, Hosanna in the highest!*

The experience of God's presence in our lives is unparalleled. It brings a sense of hope, peace, clarity, and purpose wrapped in love that fills the hearts of believers. This profound connection inspires individuals to act with compassion and kindness, which promotes camaraderie and support among those who walk in the unity of the faith, forming the body of Christ in the image that we were created to be. The weight of His glory transforms everything in the environment, causing a shift in our circumstances that leads to unrestricted praise for who He is and the expectation of what He has done, what He is doing, and what He will do.

This praise is what the people demonstrated when they shouted, "Hosanna in the highest!" as recorded in Mark 11:7-10. Their heartfelt cries reflected a deep recognition of His sovereignty and an unwavering hope for redemption. In that moment, the atmosphere was charged with faith, and the collective spirit of the crowd became a powerful witness to the positive effects of praise. "Hosanna" is a Hebrew expression meaning "save now." Those who have a covenant relationship with God can cry out to the Lord with praises and prayers, asking Him to save us in our time of need. This communal praise echoes a plea for help and reinforces the bond among believers, uniting them in their shared trust and devoutness to the Most High God. **Let us praise God!**

Hosanna

PRAISE REFLECTION

_____

_____

_____

_____

_____

_____

_____

_____

_____

_____

GLORY MOMENTS

_____

_____

_____

_____

_____

_____

_____

_____

_____

_____

Day 13

POURING PRAISE

PSALM 71:8

My mouth is filled with your praise,
declaring your splendor all day long.

There are times in our lives when we experience a lack of spiritual fulfillment. Such an experience is an opportunity for us to look to God, knowing that the emptiness is the qualification for us to be poured into, just as Jesus did with the water pot in the Gospel of John, Chapter 2. God will fill our souls with His presence. We must remain open and receptive during these moments, allowing His love to permeate our hearts. Because of this openness, we are able to have a more personal encounter with God, which results in a deeper sense of appreciation and love for Him, as well as a stronger sense of peace and love for ourselves.

Despite what seemingly appeared to be dire circumstances, the woman at the well serves as a poignant reminder. Her deliverance brought about an expression of praise that mirrored gratitude to Jesus, who met her in the midst of her spiritual dryness and poured the hope that she required into her heart. In our lives, we can be like wells from which God pours out His abundant goodness. This abundance encourages us to express from our lips the gratitude and praise to Him with love and thanksgiving. As we embrace this truth, we become conduits of His grace, sharing the living water with those around us. In doing so, we not only nourish our souls but also inspire others to seek God and experience the power that renews faith. **Let us pour out our praise to the Lord!**

Pour Out Our Praise

PRAISE REFLECTION

_____

_____

_____

_____

_____

_____

_____

_____

_____

_____

GLORY MOMENTS

_____

_____

_____

_____

_____

_____

_____

_____

_____

_____

Day 14

GIVE GOD THE GLORY

PSALM 50:23

*Whoever offers praise glorifies Me; And to
him who orders his conduct aright
I will show the salvation of God.*

As you have heard, we were created to give God glory. It is through perfect praise that we offer glory to God. The word "Perfect" in Hebrew means to make whole, sound, and complete. The Bible declares that God does not share His glory with any other god or idols. If we are not giving God the glory, then who are we sharing it with? The Psalmist informs us that when we offer Praises to God, He is glorified. This means that when we encounter situations in our lives that God helps us come through, we offer our praises and thanksgiving to Him.

In Luke 17:11-19, Jesus healed ten lepers, yet only one returned to express gratitude and glorified Him. This story highlights the importance of being thankful and recognizing the blessings we receive. It serves as a reminder that gratitude is not just an act of acknowledgment. Our praise not only shows God that we are thankful but also grateful. When such gratitude is seen in the life of the believer, the perception of the way we view God in our lives shifts, and we begin to see more opportunities to praise Him. This shift in perspective offers us the opportunity to have a significant influence on our day-to-day interactions, thus enhancing the way we relate to God and others. Learning to be grateful allows us to recognize the beauty around us and to appreciate the small moments that often go unnoticed. Today, let's pause and offer a praise of thanksgiving to God for the small moments we experience. **Let us praise God!**

Glory, Glory, Glory!

PRAISE REFLECTION

_____

_____

_____

_____

_____

_____

_____

_____

_____

_____

GLORY MOMENTS

_____

_____

_____

_____

_____

_____

_____

_____

_____

_____

Day 15

MY PRAISE IS MY WEAPON

2 Chronicles 20:22

Now when they began to sing and to praise, the Lord set ambushes against the people of Ammon, Moab, and Mount Seir, who had come against Judah; and they were defeated.

King Jehoshaphat faced threats from three nations in 2 Chronicles 20. It's remarkable how he turned directly to God, who assured him that the battle was not his to fight, but the Lord's. So, what do you do after you receive confirmation that the challenge you are dealing with belongs to God? Jehoshaphat persisted in his worship of God alongside his companions, and from this moment, a praiser emerged to offer praise to God. Will we allow our worship to bring us praise? The exuberant praise that emanated from Judah went into battle with them, causing them to win the battle. God moved on behalf of Judah and Jerusalem during their praise to God. So, we must stand firm in our praise even in battle and when things are hard.

It is essential that we clearly understand that the praise we provide is a weapon and that it battles on our behalf during trying times. This praise acts as an ally in our struggles, much like a companion in battle. When used wisely, praise to God has the ability to lift one's spirit, instill a sense of endurance, and alter even the most difficult of situations. The enemy desires nothing more than for us to remain silent, possessing a defeated mindset. But God has equipped us with everything we need to be victorious in battle and to overcome obstacles while on this life journey. Embracing this concept allows us to rise above adversity and gain a renewed hope in God. When we approach the fight with this mentality, we stay in the position of praise, giving God the glory. **Let us praise God!**

Lion of Judah

PRAISE REFLECTION

_____

_____

_____

_____

_____

_____

_____

_____

_____

_____

GLORY MOMENTS

_____

_____

_____

_____

_____

_____

_____

_____

_____

_____

Day 16

GREAT NAME

PSALM 61:8

*Then I will ever sing in praise of your name
and fulfill my vows day after day.*

Praising God really demonstrates who He is in our lives and how we see Him. Through praising God daily, we establish a connection that anchors us and reveals the greatness of His name. Having praise encounters brings about a level of clarity to the relationship that gives us the desire to pursue God even more earnestly. The more time we spend with Him, the more we experience His love and grace in our daily lives. This insight affects not just our private life but also the outside circumstances that may have an effect on our inner peace. By living out the principles He set, we become channels of His compassion and light in a world that often needs hope and encouragement.

In this Psalm David stands on God's name (a Strong Tower) while he handles his commitment to God. Sometimes, the tasks we must complete in our daily lives can be laborious, draining us of the joy that comes from God. However, when we continue in our praise while serving in our work, we become steadfast in His strength and produce melodies of praise that lighten the load and give us great joy. This joy serves as a reminder of the purpose behind our efforts, transforming our tasks into acts of worship. As we align our hearts with His will, we obtain renewed energy and inspiration, allowing our daily responsibilities to become avenues for expressing gratitude and love. This, in turn, fosters growth and joyfulness. **Let us praise God!**

Great Name

PRAISE REFLECTION

_____

_____

_____

_____

_____

_____

_____

_____

_____

_____

GLORY MOMENTS

_____

_____

_____

_____

_____

_____

_____

_____

_____

_____

Day 17

AWESOME IS HE

PSALM 68:35

You, God, are awesome in your sanctuary;
the God of Israel gives power and strength to his people.
Praise be to God!

Have you ever sat in awe of God and how majestic He is in all His ways, and how He continues to show up for us during our weakness? Have you ever encountered God's love to such an extent that His presence left you in awe? His grace envelops us, providing strength and comfort even in our most challenging moments. It gives us comfort, and it's a reminder that we are never truly alone, as His presence guides us through every trial we face. He is awesome. God does not hold back His goodness toward us, so why do we hold back from Him in times of distress? In those moments of uncertainty, we often forget to lean into that love and guidance, choosing instead to rely on our understanding. Yet, it is precisely in surrendering to His will that we discover true peace and strength.

I love the fact that David opened this Psalm with praise and concluded by still praising even though he had concerns. This approach demonstrates a profound understanding of faith and fortitude. It reminds us that expressing gratitude can coexist with our struggles, allowing us to maintain hope in uncertain times in our lives. As we cultivate a lifestyle of gratitude toward God, we start to encounter Him from various perspectives, enhancing our praise in every aspect. This holistic approach to praise encourages us to see beyond our immediate concerns and appreciate the larger picture of God's grace. God's awesomeness continues to be displayed in our lives, revealing who He is through His creations. By incorporating our praises, we eliminate worry. The practice changes our mindset and gives us strength as His presence leads our daily journey. **Let us praise God!**

Awesome God

PRAISE REFLECTION

_____

_____

_____

_____

_____

_____

_____

_____

_____

_____

GLORY MOMENTS

_____

_____

_____

_____

_____

_____

_____

_____

_____

_____

Day 18

PUT PRAISE ON IT!

2 Samuel 6:14

Wearing a linen ephod, David was dancing before the Lord
with all his might, while he and all Israel were bringing up
the ark of the Lord with shouts and the sound of trumpets.

There are about 150 instances in the Bible where the words
"thank" and "thanksgiving" are found. Not only that, but
there are about 73 passages that encourage us to express appreciation a total of 73 times. Show an attitude of thankfulness,
which is the means by which we might increase our praise. As we
praise God for the victories He gives us, it is important to "Put A
Praise on It". These words express our gratitude to God for demonstrating His mighty hand in our lives. Not only does this expression
of gratitude increase our faith, but it also inspires other believers to
acknowledge and rejoice in the benefits that they have received. By
encouraging one another and sharing our experiences, this gratitude

manifests as thankfulness, demonstrating that we do not take God for granted but rather value everything He does for us.

King David seizes this opportunity to express his gratitude to God through the joyful act of dancing. In Hebrew, the word "Karar" means "to dance," and David did not hold back from thanking God; he was not concerned about who was looking on, nor did he think about how he appeared to others, but he gave God all of himself in that moment. His actions also provoked others to express their praise. This is what we were created for: to give God all of us. Just as David's actions displayed what was in his heart, so do our actions reveal to God our hearts. The Bible informs us that "Man looks at the outer appearance, and God looks at the heart" (1 Sam. 16:7). Let our hearts reveal thanksgiving to God as we "Put a Praise on It." **Let us praise God!**

Put a Praise on It!

PRAISE REFLECTION

_____
_____
_____
_____
_____
_____
_____
_____
_____
_____

GLORY MOMENTS

_____
_____
_____
_____
_____
_____
_____
_____
_____
_____

Day 19

MIGHTY GOD

DEUTERONOMY 10:17

For the Lord your God is God of gods and Lord of lords, the great God, mighty and awesome, who shows no partiality and accepts no bribes.

In light of God's vastness in connection to our world, He undoubtedly deserves all our praise. We should express our gratitude not just through words, but also through our actions and the way we conduct our lives. Through the embodiment of love, kindness, and compassion, we showcase the greatness of His presence in our everyday interactions. Honor to God: display His mighty influence and deeds in the lives of the devoted. We navigate the most challenging situations we encounter through God. Embracing a life of gratitude goes beyond simple acknowledgment; it is a transformative journey that embodies our core values of love, kindness, and compassion.

Through our words and actions of gratitude, we elevate those around us and reveal the profound presence of God in our lives.

Every interaction presents a chance to demonstrate His grace, particularly during challenges when faith serves as our guiding light. In the end, embracing a heart filled with gratitude allows us to maneuver through life's intricacies while consistently acknowledging the divine presence that guides our journeys. By committing ourselves to the expression of gratitude to God, our praise motivates others and cultivates a community rooted in faith and strength. Considering the immense nature of God in relation to our world, He truly merits all our gratitude. Glory to God: showcase His powerful hand and actions in the lives of the faithful. It is through God that we navigate the most challenging situations we encounter and become overcomers. **Let us praise God!**

Lord You Mighty

PRAISE REFLECTION

_____

_____

_____

_____

_____

_____

_____

_____

_____

_____

GLORY MOMENTS

_____

_____

_____

_____

_____

_____

_____

_____

_____

_____

Day 20

RENEWED PRAISE

PSALMS 51:12

*Restore to me the joy of your salvation and
grant me a willing spirit, to sustain me.*

There are times in life when we don't worship God as often as we should, yet no matter where we are, He is still exalted. In those moments of doubt or distance, it's important to remember the joy of our salvation and the place God met us with His love that covered us in our weakness. Through His presence, we embrace His joy, which refreshes our praise and causes us to display a thankful attitude toward God. Ultimately, navigating moments of doubt and distance does not diminish the unwavering exaltation of God, which transcends any physical location. In times of uncertainty, reflecting on the joy of salvation and the depth of God's love serves as a powerful reminder of His unchanging nature. By actively embracing God's presence, individuals can revitalize their praise and cultivate a spirit of thankfulness. This ongoing practice enhances the praise experience while also reinforcing our relationship with God, grounding us in a profound understanding that even in the midst of struggles, God's glory remains ever-present and worthy of adoration.

Though the Psalmist found himself in a time of despair, he knew that approaching God with a broken spirit and a contrite heart would draw God near to him. In this state, we must adopt a humble attitude that will bring us closer to God and enable us to offer praise. The Psalmist's transformation shows that even in our worst circumstances, humility can deepen our relationship with God and help us see His love. The Psalmist's journey shows how despair and devotion come together, reminding us that our troubles can lead to faith and appreciation. **Let us praise God!**

River of The Lord

PRAISE REFLECTION

_____

_____

_____

_____

_____

_____

_____

_____

_____

_____

GLORY MOMENTS

_____

_____

_____

_____

_____

_____

_____

_____

_____

_____

Day 21

MIGHTY WORKS

ISAIAH 55:12

*You will go out in joy and be led forth in peace; the
mountains and hills will burst into song before you,
and all the trees of the field will clap their hands.*

G od's creation has witnessed and experienced his mighty
work upon the earth, and it is fascinating to observe how
the birds of the air and the trees react to this work. This
highlights the beauty and harmony found in nature as a reflection
of God's creative power that leads us into offering him praise. The
complicated fabric of nature stands as a testament to God's mag-
nificent handiwork, where every bird's song and every rustling leaf
echoes the divine craftsmanship that brought them into existence.
This harmonious interplay among the elements of creation not only
illustrates the profound connection between God and the natural
world but also serves as a reminder of the beauty that surrounds us.

As we observe the splendor of our environment, we are drawn to acknowledge and celebrate God's creative power, recognizing that it invites us to appreciate life in all its forms. This acknowledgment encourages us to cultivate a sense of gratitude towards God's wonders, and we experience his work in nature. Ultimately, nature's beauty becomes a source of inspiration and praise, urging us to honor the artistry of creation and fostering a deeper reverence for God in the world we inhabit.

It is truly captivating to observe how God selected humanity to reflect his image, where beauty and splendor mirror his powerful creations, resulting in the praise that is meant to harmonize with the works He has done. As God-created work brings forth songs of praise that exalt Him, we must continue to recognize our role in this divine symphony. By embracing our unique gifts and talents, we contribute to a collective expression of gratitude that resonates throughout all of creation. **Let us praise God!**

Hallelujah!!!

PRAISE REFLECTION

_____
_____
_____
_____
_____
_____
_____
_____
_____
_____

GLORY MOMENTS

_____
_____
_____
_____
_____
_____
_____
_____
_____
_____

Day 22

LIFTED PRAISE

PSALMS 145:1-2

My heart explodes with praise to you! Now and forever my heart bows in worship to you, my King and my God! Every day I will lift my praise to your name with praises that will last throughout eternity.

Praise to God is so powerful that it draws in His presence to lift you out of what I call "a stuck place," emotionally, spiritually, or physically, bringing about a joy that resonates from the innermost part of your being. This joy, which emanates from deep within, transforms your state of being and provides a sense of freedom and renewal. By engaging in heartfelt praise, you invite God's intervention that can help you overcome challenges and obstacles in your life. The overcoming of these obstacles brings about exalted praise to God, thus releasing a level of thanksgiving that is unmatched by the circumstances we are faced with. This unmatched level of thanksgiving reflects a profound spiritual connection that we have with God and transcends everyday struggles, allowing for a greater appreciation of life's blessings. Your faith strengthens as you celebrate these victories, reinforcing the cycle of praise and gratitude.

We continue to overcome our struggles by expressing praises that exalt God, realigning our focus on him. Have you ever watched an individual walk an elevated tightrope? One thing that is crucial is that their focus is not on what's around them, but on what is ahead of them. They are not concerned about failure but expect success. This is what giving praise to God does; it assists us with staying grounded in our faith and encourages us to move forward with confidence. By maintaining a perspective of gratitude, we can navigate life's challenges with a sense of purpose and hope, trusting that we are supported in our journey. We lift our praises to God as He guides us through various situations. **Let us praise God!**

God's Got Me

PRAISE REFLECTION

_____

_____

_____

_____

_____

_____

_____

_____

_____

GLORY MOMENTS

_____

_____

_____

_____

_____

_____

_____

_____

_____

Day 23

STANDING PRAISE

NEHEMIAH 9:5

And the Levites—Jeshua, Kadmiel, Bani, Hashabneiah, Sherebiah, Hodiah, Shebaniah and Pethahiah—said: "Stand up and praise the Lord your God, who is from everlasting to everlasting. "Blessed be your glorious name, and may it be exalted above all blessing and praise."

I t is healthy for the body of Christ when leaders are standing, giving God praise. The vitality of leaders praising and worshiping God leads the people into the presence of God, increasing faith and unity among the Christian community. This collective worship cultivates an atmosphere of encouragement and support, empowering members to grow their relationship with God. As leaders model this devotion, it inspires others to engage wholeheartedly in their spiritual journeys, creating a vibrant and thriving church environment. In such an environment, we become more unified with God and each other, strengthening our relationships. When we unite in praise to God, it extends beyond the church's four walls into the community, where we share our faith and serve others beyond the church.

Nehemiah 9:5 emphasizes the significance of following true repentance with praise to God for His goodness. This highlights the importance of expressing gratitude and worship as a natural response to genuine repentance, reinforcing the connection between our faith and communal worship. Such praise not only honors God but also brings unity and purpose within the church and the wider community. The Levites' vision for praise within the community serves as a powerful reminder of the essential elements that unite us in faith and service. **Let us praise God!**

Lion

PRAISE REFLECTION

_____

_____

_____

_____

_____

_____

_____

_____

_____

_____

GLORY MOMENTS

_____

_____

_____

_____

_____

_____

_____

_____

_____

_____

Day 24

GARMENT OF PRAISE

ISAIAH 61:3

And provide for those who grieve in Zion to bestow on them a crown of beauty instead of ashes, the oil of joy instead of mourning, and a garment of praise instead of a spirit of despair. They will be called oaks of righteousness, a planting of the Lord for the display of his splendor.

O n this Christian journey, we discover ourselves dealing with grief for diverse reasons. Every experience influences our perception of love and loss. As we journey through these difficult emotions, it is important to recognize the distinct ways in which grief impacts our lives. In this text, the term "grief" is used interchangeably with "mourning," which refers to experiencing profound sorrow. This definition emphasizes the emotional weight of grief, highlighting that it can arise from various circumstances. Grief is not limited to the loss of a loved one but can stem from a range of life changes and challenges.

It is truly remarkable that God acknowledges our sorrow and intervenes for a transformation. We sometimes struggle with trusting God when it comes to letting go of various emotions. In this verse, it is evident that God does not take from us without offering something in return. Isaiah conveys that God desires to bestow upon us the garment of praise in exchange for our grief and despair. God demonstrates that His intention for praise in a believer's life should remain unaffected by any circumstance. His intention for a life filled with praise remains steadfast, reminding us that even in our darkest moments, there is an opportunity for us to praise God.

I Believe

PRAISE REFLECTION

_____

_____

_____

_____

_____

_____

_____

_____

_____

GLORY MOMENTS

_____

_____

_____

_____

_____

_____

_____

_____

_____

Day 25

ELEVATED PRAISE

PSALM 106:1

Praise the Lord Give thanks to the Lord,
for he is good; his love endures forever.

E levated praise to God brings you into a state of recognition and appreciation, enhancing your confidence and motivation. This acknowledgment inspires you to pursue further achievements and foster a positive mindset. Elevated praise helps us overcome hurdles by emphasizing appreciation and respect, which increases our spiritual strength and clarity when overcoming life's setbacks. This positive outlook gives you the strength to be determined and purposeful even when things are difficult. Elevated praise to God inspires us to reach new heights and motivates us to stay on the path that God has intended for our lives.

The first verse of Psalm 106 expresses the Psalmist's high adoration for the presence of God as well as the wonderful works that were brought about by trust in God. This deep respect expressed through praise to God not only fortifies our faith but also encourages us to reflect on the blessings we frequently take for granted. This sentiment is beautifully reflected in the fact that it begins with heartfelt gratitude that acknowledges the goodness of the Lord. This gratitude serves as a reminder of the numerous blessings that help us acquire the courage to overcome obstacles, giving God praise and walking in divine purposes, and reinforcing the importance of celebrating His presence in our lives. **Let us praise God!**

The Blessing

PRAISE REFLECTION

_____

_____

_____

_____

_____

_____

_____

_____

_____

GLORY MOMENTS

_____

_____

_____

_____

_____

_____

_____

_____

_____

Day 26

MOVING PRAISE

PSALM 100:4

Enter his gates with thanksgiving, and his courts with praise.
Give thanks to him; bless his name!

We have a manner in which we come to God when we offer Him our praise. The elements presented in the verse illustrate how the Psalmist urges us to cultivate a thankful heart that should accompany our praise. The term "praise" in the verse refers to the word "Thillah," which signifies "to sing." The verse instructs us to offer a melody to God as we approach His presence. In biblical times, it was essential to bring gifts when approaching a king, as a sign of respect and honor in their presence. We understand even more that God is the King of kings and the Lord of lords (Revelation 17:14) when we bring Him our praise. In doing this, our praise honors God. The term "bless" in the verse is represented by the word "Barak," which signifies bowing or bending knees in a gesture of adoration.

Moving praise is a continuous process that is displayed from an intentional heart. This enables us to actively demonstrate to God the glory that is due to His name. In doing so, we experience His presence that offers us peace, comfort, love, joy, and protection simultaneously. Praising God isn't just a nod to His greatness; it's like sending an RSVP to a divine connection that spices up our spiritual journey! This continuous act of adoration cultivates a feeling of fulfillment and heavenly confidence in our lives, and when we do not cast off our confidence, we receive rewards from God (Hebrews 10:35). This allows us to testify of the goodness of God to others and give hope to those in whom God put in our pathway. **Let us praise God!**

He's A Wonder

PRAISE REFLECTION

_____

_____

_____

_____

_____

_____

_____

_____

_____

GLORY MOMENTS

_____

_____

_____

_____

_____

_____

_____

_____

_____

Day 27

PRAISE NOT ANOTHER

PSALM 115:1

*Not to us, Lord, not to us but to your name be the
glory, because of your love and faithfulness.*

At times, we find ourselves in situations that lead us to misdirect our praise and extend it to someone else. It poses a risk for believers to elevate themselves and their achievements while placing ultimate praise on another for their role in the healing process. While it is important to express gratitude to others, ultimately, all honor belongs to God. Here we celebrate our God and the ways He supports us in all circumstances. It is important to acknowledge that God is the source of the resources we have in our lives. As we acknowledge God as our divine support, He deeply weaves His resources into our life journey, leading to the praise that emerges from the depths of our being. This illustrates the importance of gratitude in our lives.

As we navigate this path, it is crucial to remain humble, avoiding the pitfalls of self-elevation that can obscure our vision and diminish our appreciation for the guidance we receive. By acknowledging God's faithfulness as a constant source of strength and resources, we cultivate a more significant bond with God and our faith while increasing our experiences. Adopting this viewpoint inspires us to convey sincere appreciation, nurturing a sense of humility that reveres God through our acts of praise. Ultimately, acknowledging God's presence in our journey fosters an immense feeling of peacefulness and vitality that surpasses obstacles. When we recognize God as our source, it helps us keep our focus on Him and gives glory to His name as we enjoy His blessings. **Let us praise God!**

Yahweh!

PRAISE REFLECTION

_____

_____

_____

_____

_____

_____

_____

_____

_____

GLORY MOMENTS

_____

_____

_____

_____

_____

_____

_____

_____

_____

Day 28

PROTECTED PRAISE

PROVERBS 4:23

Above all else, guard your heart, for everything you do flows from it.

Keeping continual praise to God is vital, and we must understand that praise should be a lifestyle for believers. Embracing a lifestyle of continuous praise to God is not merely an optional practice for believers; it is essential for spiritual growth and fulfillment. This ongoing expression of thankfulness and reverence to God enhances both individual faith and communal worship, therefore creating a shield against discouragement and safeguarding your praise. This shield against discouragement refers to the protective effect that constant praise can have on a believer's mindset, helping them remain hopeful and resilient in challenging times. By prioritizing praise, our gratitude allows us to stand reflecting the glory of God. This reflection not only illuminates God, but it also speaks to our current situation, bringing about a resolve.

The writer of Proverbs 4:23 urges us to protect our hearts, as it is the foundation of our emotions and the source of our praise. By safeguarding your heart, you are also safeguarding your ability to praise. In this way, we provide genuine praise to God, free from the constraints of routine. This intentional safeguarding allows us to rise above the ordinary limitations that frequently hinder worship, allowing us to convey true and heartfelt gratitude that is both spontaneous and sincere. This practice leads us into a genuine expression of love for God without any hindrance. **Let us praise God!**

Let The Praise Begin

PRAISE REFLECTION

_____

_____

_____

_____

_____

_____

_____

_____

_____

GLORY MOMENTS

_____

_____

_____

_____

_____

_____

_____

_____

_____

Day 29

CONTAGIOUS PRAISE

PSALM 95:1-2

Come, let us sing for joy to the Lord; let us shout aloud to the Rock of our salvation. Let us come before him with thanksgiving and extol him with music and song.

Psalms 95:1–2 informs us to give thanks to God without holding back by being thankful and remembering the day He saved us. This invitation to worship invites us to open our hearts and voices, recognizing His greatness and mercy. As we come together in unity, our joyful expressions echo, inviting others to join us in the expression of their praise to God. When this begins to happen, it creates a powerful atmosphere of worship that transcends individual experiences. Praising God in the presence of others ignites a spark. Every individual transforms into a glowing ember as we contemplate the goodness of God. When the ember reaches its peak and the wind picks up, it breaks off and ignites another fire, seizing the dry patches and making containment difficult.

Likewise, our praise of God spreads within communal environments and uplifts the spirits of those who might be feeling spiritually parched. Living an engaging life can drain your energy, leaving you feeling empty, yet it is praise that sustains your vibrancy even in times of despair. The transforming power of praise to God serves as an inspiration of hope. In moments of uncertainty, this praise can galvanize individuals to come together, which promotes a sense of solidarity and purpose. It serves as a reminder that even in our most challenging times, there is illumination to be discovered in united faith and shared appreciation. In the end, embracing the power of praise elevates the spirit and nurtures a sense of intertwining us to become one in the body of Christ, cultivating an environment where faith flourishes and thrives. **Let us praise God!**

Contagious Praise

PRAISE REFLECTION

_____

_____

_____

_____

_____

_____

_____

_____

_____

GLORY MOMENTS

_____

_____

_____

_____

_____

_____

_____

_____

_____

Day 30

GOD GREAT GOD

PSALMS 95:3-7

For the LORD is the great God, the great King above all gods. In his hand are the depths of the earth, and the mountain peaks belong to him. The sea is his, for he made it, and his hands formed the dry land.

The magnificence of God stands unparalleled by anyone or anything. The ways of God are majestic and surpass our thoughts and imaginations. The greatness of God has been evident since the dawn of time, showcased in His ability to take something without purpose and impart it meaning as He crafted creation over seven days. This is truly remarkable. God specializes in giving purpose to what he created. Psalm 139:14 reveals that we were fearfully and wonderfully made by God, while Isaiah 43:7 expresses His purpose, stating, "everyone who is called by my name, whom I created for my glory, whom I formed and made." So far, we observe that God has created us for His glory, and we reverence Him by proclaiming praises to Him, as stated in Isaiah 43:21: "The people I formed for myself, that they may proclaim my praise." Appreciation is fundamental to our way of life; this is what God desires from all of creation.

God allows us to experience His signs and wonders so that we will continue our praise to Him. Through the lens of faith, we come to understand that God's allowance for praise serves as a powerful conduit for experiencing His signs and wonders in our lives. Each moment of praise and worship opens our eyes to His divine presence that surrounds us, revealing the exceptional in the ordinary. This ongoing practice of praise enhances our relationship with God. We experience God's manifest love and grace, urging us to celebrate His goodness with every breath we take. **Let us praise God!**

God Great God

PRAISE REFLECTION

_____

_____

_____

_____

_____

_____

_____

_____

_____

GLORY MOMENTS

_____

_____

_____

_____

_____

_____

_____

_____

_____

Here is the compiled list of songs on Spotify featured in this book. Access is available by scanning the QR Code..

Power of Praise